Moose

Moose

DANIEL WOOD

Whitecap Books

Vancouver / Toronto / New York

The information in this book is true and complete to the best of our knowledge. All recommendations are made without guarantee on the part of the author or Whitecap Books Ltd. The author and publisher disclaim any liability in connection with the use of this information. For additional information please contact Whitecap Books Ltd., 351 Lynn Avenue, North Vancouver, BC V7J 2C4. Information on this and other Whitecap titles can also be found at the Whitecap web site: <www.whitecap.ca>.

Edited by Elaine Jones
Proofread by Elizabeth McLean
Cover design by Steve Penner
Interior design by Margaret Ng
Desktop publishing by Susan Greenshields
Cover photograph by Tim Christie

Printed in Canada.

Canadian Cataloguing in Publication Data

Wood, Daniel.
    Moose

        Includes bibliographical references and index.
        ISBN 1-55110-950-6

        1. Moose. I. Title.
QL737.U55W66 1999   599.65'7   C99-910844-1

The moose is singularly grotesque and awkward to look at . . .
a great frightened rabbit with long ears.
—Henry David Thoreau

In all the vast region that is dotted on my map,
the moose is, or was . . . the staff of life.
—Ernest Thompson Seton

PREVIOUS PAGES: *When American explorers Meriwether Lewis and William Clark crossed the northern U.S. in their famous 1803–1806 expedition, they encountered no moose. The reason: there were none in the region. In the last 150 years, however, the animal has spread south from Canada along the forested corridor of the Rocky Mountains and now inhabits seven western states. Here a cow browses in early autumn below Wyoming's Grand Teton Mountains.*

C O N T E N T S

INTRODUCTION

THE MOOSE—A SYMBOL OF SURVIVAL IN A COLD PLACE

Throughout the tangled boreal forests of the northern hemisphere, wherever the spruce and pine and aspen run out and the wooded darkness yields to boggy oases of sunlight, there exists the possibility of a silent apparition appearing. Some say it's comic. Some say it's droll. Others have called it ugly or Zen-like. But when a moose, especially a big male, moves out of the shadows of the forest's margins, it stands as a chimerical emblem of nature's ability to surprise. For the moose is the last survivor of the huge, extinct Pleistocene creatures—the mammoth, the cow-sized giant sloth, the saber-toothed tiger, the Irish elk with its 4-metre (13-foot) antlers—that once populated the North.

No one has ever accused the moose of being pretty or astute. Its detractors have said it looks like an animal made of spare parts. This may explain its widespread appeal.

PREVIOUS PAGE, LEFT: *By mid-September, the antlers of this bull have shed their velvet in preparation for the fall rut. The boreal forest is full of pheromones as the males battle for supremacy, displaying their antlers in endless head-wagging, strutting, snorting, and occasional pushing matches. The bulls don't eat for three weeks and may lose 20 percent of their weight during this time of conflict. Here a bull rests after a rutting fight.*

PREVIOUS PAGE, RIGHT: *To most observers, the moose's mismatched and oversized features give it comic appeal. The olfactory powers of the gargantuan nose compensate for the animal's beady and somewhat myopic eyes. The size of the bull's beard, or dewlap, varies greatly from animal to animal, and its massive antlers have sexual significance to the cows.*

Its eyes are weak and beady. Upwind from a suspected intruder, the moose simply stands motionlessly and gawks. Its bulbous nose is effective for smelling, but so large it half-drapes, like that of Disney's Goofy, over its lower lip. The male moose's top-heavy, palmated antlers, growing sidewards from its knobby cranium, may reach a weight of 36 kilograms (80 pounds). Its enormous, rabbit-like ears can— and *do*—pivot 360 degrees when the animal senses danger. Below its chin hangs a drooping flap of skin and hair called a dewlap that, on some males, dangles a metre (39 inches) down to the knees. It serves absolutely no purpose known to science. The moose has the legs of a ballerina, long and elegant, but these support the muscled chest of a steroid-enhanced wrestler. Its tail is a stunted stub. These physical

LEFT: *In this typical family portrait, a cow and her offspring eye a wilderness stranger. One of the great surprises for backcountry travelers—kayaking a northern B.C. river, hiking in the Colorado Rockies, canoeing an Ontario lake, driving a logging road in Alaska—is the sudden realization that the visitor is being watched. Since moose do not fear humans, the human intruders have time to savor the wilderness epiphany.*

features, its impressive size, and its stoic manner have endeared the animal to millions of people whose only contact with a moose is reading Dr. Seuss's *Thidwick the Big-Hearted Moose* or drinking New Hampshire's Two Moose beer.

For the Native peoples of North America's boreal forests—that vast, continent-wide expanse of conifers that stretches northward to the treeline in Canada and southward to the deciduous woods of the United States—the moose was the primary animal upon which their lives depended. Like the buffalo to the Plains Indians and the salmon to the Native peoples of the Pacific Northwest, the moose acquired a near-mythic status among the Algonquin of New England, the Ojibway of Ontario, the Shoshone of Wyoming, and people of Alaska's Bering Strait. It was more than sustenance, more than hide for moccasins or sinew for thread or hoofs for ceremonial rattles. For millennia, the moose—from the Algonquin word *moosu,* meaning "he strips off young tree bark"—was the difference between life and death for many people of the North. It is the world's largest living member of the deer family and the largest antlered creature ever to exist. Reaching heights among the Alaskan subspecies of 2.5 metres (8 feet) and weights of 820 kilograms (1800 pounds), it shares with the buffalo and grizzly the distinction of being the biggest wild animal on the North American continent.

According to the legends of the Abenaki of Maine, the very first moose were so huge people couldn't hunt them. So the benevolent Great Spirit squished the animal downward, explaining its odd proportions, humped back, flattened antlers, and bulging nose. The Micmacs of Nova Scotia explained the moose's affinity for water by saying the animal

originated in the sea. In dreams, a moose was seen as a harbinger of a long life. And in hunts, the big, benign creature was treated with tremendous respect because it furnished a cornucopia of meat, skin, fur, and bone. But the moose, unlike the grizzly or coyote, assumed no mystical role in Aboriginal thinking. It was not perceived as fear-inspiring or shrewd. It was instead provident; it provided for the future.

The early European settlers of North America were familiar with the moose because three of the seven subspecies worldwide live on the Eurasian landmass. (Sweden, in fact, has the highest density of moose on earth.) The colonists carried with them their own, sometimes comic myths about the gigantic creature. They said its left hind foot, powdered and drunk with wine, cured epilepsy. Its dried nerves cured arthritis. They said it used its scoop-shaped antlers to plow a path through winter snow. It was also believed moose loved the sound of music. One apocryphal 19th-century story from Scandinavia reported that a hunter hired a violinist to play in order to lure a moose within shooting range, but that the moose was so annoyed by the violin's sound, it charged the two intruders and killed them. When Europeans arrived in North America armed with rifles, the moose came off less well. By 1875, the human population had eradicated moose from most of New England and the states bordering the Great Lakes. It was only in the nearly impenetrable, unpopulated vastness of Canada and Alaska that the moose prevailed.

Today, the moose is reoccupying its old haunts along the northern U.S. border and spreading southward along the Rockies as far as Utah. But except in Alaska, it's rare that a traveler, even a back-country hiker, will see the elusive animal. It lives, by and large, alone,

LEFT: *To the 60 000 semi-nomadic Native people who lived in northern North America before the arrival of Europeans, the moose was one of the primary sources of clothing, tools, and sustenance. Along with deer and fish, moose meat meant life to many early peoples. Ethnozoologists estimate that a band of 100 people could have subsisted for a year on the meat of 142 moose; its nutritional equivalence would be 949 butchered deer.*

PREVIOUS PAGE: *The life of a moose cow is made more difficult in winter. This Canadian cow, her muzzle dusted with snow, faces several challenges: an 80 percent reduction in forage once northern plant life dies off; deep snow; the ongoing care of her inexperienced offspring; and the possibility of being newly pregnant.*

existing in the wilderness amid mosquito-infested swampland where few human intruders go. Its usual occupation during those summer months when most people are outdoors is standing thigh-deep in a beaver pond or marsh munching on half-submerged pond weed, then retreating to a shaded copse for an hour's quiet rumination on the vegetation it has ingested. It seldom moves far from home. So it is that, wherever there's a boggy clearing in the boreal spruce and pine, there's a place with HMP—high moose potential. At these locations, a visitor can wait and wait, stare and stare, hoping for a wilderness epiphany. In journalist John McPhee's resonant description, such a moment is alive with the "stillness of a moose intending to appear." It seldom, in fact, happens. But when a moose *does* appear—seen at twilight perhaps: a tall, wary mother trailed by her gangly, fuzzball calf, the two silhouetted against the pale, evanescent silver of a northern swamp—it is like hearing the evening call of a loon. The moose conjures the essential North: its emptiness, its loneliness, its relentless demands.

LEFT: *A moose cow emerges from scouring the bottom of frigid Wonder Lake, beneath Alaska's Mount McKinley. Between May and early September in most of their North American range, moose are seldom far from water, avoiding summer's bugs and eating aquatic plants.*

LEFT: *The moose, unlike several other species of deer, is not a gregarious, herding animal. Its preference, generally, is solitude and its presence is seldom observed. Because it tends to inhabit remote boreal forests and muskeg, it has never succumbed to human predation over widespread areas like the bison, whale, grizzly, or cougar. At the end of the 20th century, the moose's continent-wide population is believed to be the same—about one million—as it was 400 years ago, when Europeans first colonized North America.*

RIGHT: *This half-grown moose calf wanders the autumn shoreline of Sand Stream Pond in Maine's Baxter State Park shortly after dawn. For their first 14 months, the young are doted on by their mothers. (The fathers have no parental role.) The cows teach their offspring about food sources, predators, and the challenges of survival. Still, in some regions of North America, over 50 percent of moose calves die before they're one year old.*

RIGHT: *The moose is a ruminant, which means it initially swallows its food unchewed. The coarse vegetation is stored temporarily in a lobe of the four-part stomach called the rumen, where it begins to stew. The food next moves to the reticulum, where it's turned into pulp. Then the cud is regurgitated for some relentless grinding at 82 chews a minute before the food is finally reswallowed and digested.*

ABOVE: *Two macho moose perform a rhythmic rutting dance to display to each other—and perhaps a female nearby—their huge antlers. While prehistoric North American moose produced antlers of 2.5 metres (8 feet), today's big game trophy record is 1.95 metres (6 1/2 feet)—for an animal shot near McGrath, Alaska.*

LEFT: *By late August, prior to the annual rut, the blood flow to the antlers of this Alaskan bull has abruptly stopped, the soft covering of velvet has dried, and the skin has begun to peel off. This process — aided by the moose's "horning" its antlers against tree branches, bushes, and dirt— takes just one or two days.*

RIGHT: *During the last 150 000 years, several waves of ice age moose used the periodic Bering Strait land bridge to cross the 90-kilometre-wide (56-mile) Bering Strait between Siberia and Alaska. The gradual dispersal of moose across North America—and the subsequent arrival of Aboriginal hunters following the same route—meant the first people had a readily available supply of food. One adult moose yields over 345 kilograms (759 pounds) of dressed meat, six times more than a deer.*

LEFT: *A cow leads her young through the marshland of British Columbia's premier canoe route, Bowron Lake Provincial Park. Unlike their caribou cousins, moose generally don't migrate if the foraging is sufficient. They tend to spend their entire lives in one place. During the animal's slow, millenia-long occupation of boreal North America, four distinct subspecies have evolved. Curiously, it has been only in the last century or two that moose have inhabited the Bowron Lake region of central B.C., as well as Labrador, Newfoundland, and the western U.S.*

RIGHT: *Moose cows seek a secluded spot in late May or early June to give birth. These six-week-old* Alces alces shirasi *twins from the American Rockies spend their first months in constant contact with their hyper-vigilant mother. They'll suckle for four or five months. Intruders, whether humans or wildlife predators, have to deal with a ferocious, kick-boxing 364-kilogram (800-pound) cow.*

ABOVE: *Few images are more symbolic of the North than a moose's enormous antler rack. The bleached bones decorate thousands of garages, lakeside cabins, barns, and gateposts across the northern half of the continent. These antlers rest in the shallow water of Main Brook, Newfoundland.*

RIGHT: *Of all the creatures of the North, few are as well adapted to the virtually uninhabitable muskeg of Alaska, the Yukon, Northwest Territories, and Nunavut as the moose. Its long legs allow it to move through the region's hummocky, boglike terrain. It suffers little even in extreme cold. It thrives in stunted boreal forests of black spruce, willow, Labrador tea, and lichens.*

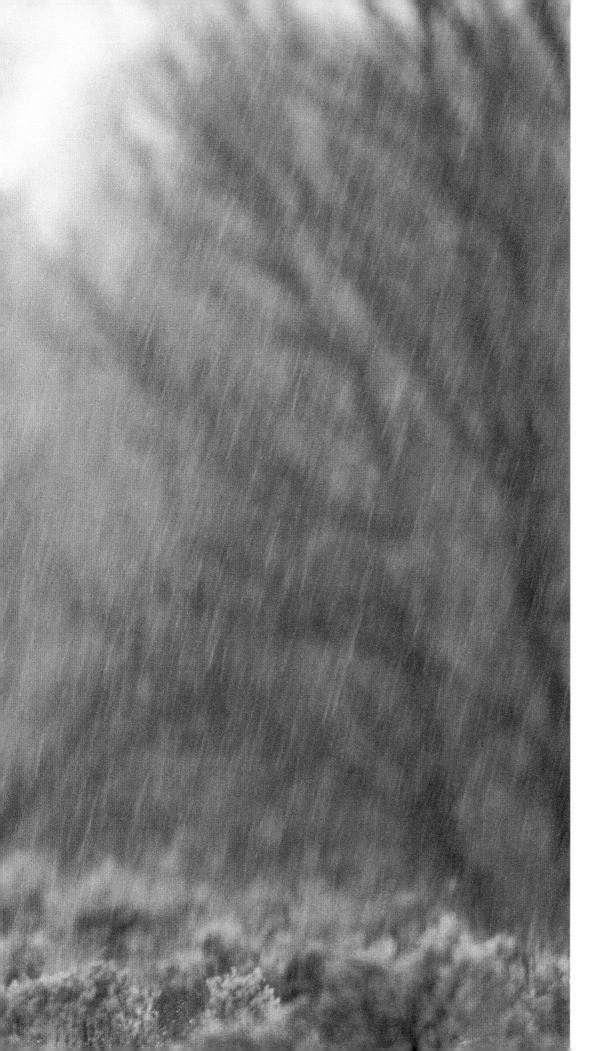

LEFT: *This rutting Wyoming bull considers a nearby competitor during an early fall snowstorm. Among moose, researchers report, size does count. Contenders for the estrous females almost always yield to the bull with the biggest set of antlers. In just 3 percent of male rutting matches does one of the combatants suffer a fatal injury. Usually, the animals inflict only minor puncture wounds to their opponents' shoulders.*

RIGHT: *Beaver and moose are natural allies, something the continent's oldest business, the 330-year-old Hudson's Bay Company, tacitly acknowledged on its coat of arms, where both animals appear. For centuries, the beaver meant fur and the moose meant meat for fur trappers. Today, as the dam-building beaver returns to the North after its extirpation from much of the continent, it is inevitably followed by the docile, pond-loving moose.*

MOOSE COUNTRY

A SOLITARY WANDERER OF THE WILDERNESS

During the periodic ice age appearances of a Bering Strait land bridge, a number of big animals, such as the grizzly and mammoth, crossed from Siberia to Alaska and found a continent open to invasion: a New World of food and prey. The moose, too, left the taiga of its Eurasian cousins behind 150 000 years ago and encountered in North America a place, if not of milk and honey, of twigs and tubers. And few predators. The animal gradually spread south and east and occupied a coast-to-coast range between the 50th and 65th parallels of latitude, an area that originally excluded southern British Columbia, the Canadian grassland prairies, and the Newfoundland-Labrador region. In the last 150 years, the post-glacial, continental dispersal of the moose has continued. It now occupies much of British Columbia, easternmost Canada, and a narrow finger of habitat that runs deep into the United States along the Rocky Mountains. The

PREVIOUS PAGE, LEFT: *This Alaskan bull, like other members of its species, spends the long hours of late summer in bouts of near-motionless rumination. With no upper incisors—only a calloused pad—the moose finds a shaded spot, kneels down, yawns a few times, and then begins grinding its cud. It presses its lower teeth against the upper pad, slowly pulverizing the fibrous vegetation it has regurgitated into a mushy, malodorous pulp.*

PREVIOUS PAGE, RIGHT: *Lip curling, known scientifically as* flehmen, *exposes a gland in the bull's palate that allows it to determine precisely the direction and reproductive susceptibility of nearby estrous females. Here a rutting male in Wyoming's Grand Teton Mountains tries to catch a whiff of "eau-de-cow."*

animal's spread southward has been limited, however, by its preference for a cool climate. Unlike other members of the deer family, moose actually become uncomfortable when temperatures rise above 14°C (57°F) and seek relief in an invigorating, cold bog-bath.

This incremental spread of moose over the millennia has produced four distinct subspecies in the animal's 9 000 000-square-kilometre (3 500 000-square-mile) North American range. The largest of these subspecies is the almost jet-black Alaska-Yukon moose (*Alces alces gigas*). Mature *A. a. gigas* bulls average 2 metres (6 1/2 feet) in height with monstrous antlers of the same horizontal width. The smallest subspecies is the mahogany-brown eastern moose (*Alces alces americana*), which lives in the Canadian provinces east of Hudson Bay and the forests of the

LEFT: *As the colorful, stunted berry bushes of the Yukon flame out in the dying weeks of September, a big bull faces the taiga and the onset of winter. The brief, vibrant period of autumn socializing, fighting, and mating will soon come to an end and 11 months of near-solitude lie ahead.*

bordering American states. The third subspecies is the greyish Wyoming moose (*Alces alces shirasi*). Its territory is limited to the states of the northern Rockies and its total numbers don't reach more than 25 000. The most widespread and populous subspecies is the brownish-black, medium-sized northwestern moose (*Alces alces andersoni*), which inhabits all of forested Canada between British Columbia and the Great Lakes, and north into the Northwest Territories and Nunavut.

Unlike most species of deer, the taciturn moose prefers territory shunned by most animals. In the bleak, black fly–infested muskeg of the Northwest Territories' Barren Grounds, along the alluvial fans of frigid Alaskan rivers, amid the stunted spruce of central Newfoundland, it goes alone. Normally, it doesn't herd. In its entire life span of 25 years, it may never — if the foraging is good — travel a half-day's walk from where it was born. [The exception to this is the famous Vagabond Moose of the American Midwest. In 1976, the itinerant bull began heading south from Minnesota's Lake Superior shore, apparently looking for a mate. In a three-year trek, the misdirected moose passed through Minnesota, Iowa, and most of Missouri before coming to loveless grief 2400 kilometres (1500 miles) from the nearest female moose.]

Generally, the moose wanders slowly, silently, and solitarily along the forest's edge, its head swinging from side to side, nibbling intermittently for 10 hours a day on the nutritious springtime buds. Later, it will eat the leaves of feltleaf willow and Sitka alder, and by midsummer it may spend those hours vacuuming underwater lily stems from the detritus of a muddy bog. During these seasons of plenty, a mature male may eat

PREVIOUS PAGE: *In Alaska's Denali National Park, early winter has arrived. By mid-December, the bulls have dropped their antlers. Both sexes have grown a thick fur that will sustain them through the cold, almost perpetually dark winter. Body temperatures decline and movements slow. Of the adult moose that die in Alaska, a third succumb—many in the winter— to the state's three major wild predators: wolves, black bears, and grizzlies.*

23 kilograms (50 pounds) of vegetation a day. These sessions of gorging are broken by more hours of sedentary chewing on its regurgitated cud. With its legs curled beneath it and its eyelids closed in stupefied moose-bliss, the animal's only visible movements are the relentless sideward reiteration of its lower jaw and its ears flicking flies. If the surrounding browse is good, it may not move from that one location for two weeks.

When it moves, however, it's a picture of slow-motion fluidity. It is seldom hurried. It doesn't usually dart or leap like smaller deer; it flows. An adult's size and potentially lethal kicks have insulated it from intimidation by most predators, except those armed with rifles. Research in Alaska has shown that two-thirds of

LEFT: *In the nearly monochromatic spruce forest of Alberta's Jasper National Park, a lone moose patrols a snowy shoreline. Throughout its range, the species naturally spreads itself out, seeking those places in winter that offer shallow snow or icy surfaces for quick escape from predators. In much of North America, the average range of a moose is only 13 square kilometres (5 square miles); in the far North, where vegetation is more sparse, a moose may have a range 25 times as large.*

young moose calves succumb to predation from bears and wolves before they reach their first birthday. Adult moose are most likely to die in winter when wolf packs can surround them in deep, crusted snow. Winter weather forces many moose, as well, onto cleared highways and train tracks, where fatalities regularly occur. In a recent British Columbia study, research indicated that several hundred moose die annually in that province when struck by trains during winter storms. But the moose's primary predator is, as it has been for centuries, its old nemesis *Homo sapiens*. To many northern residents, one of the essential autumn preparations for the months ahead is a side of moose in the freezer. It means subsistence in hundreds of places where winter darkness is seemingly endless and work scarce.

Despite these hazards, the moose—like many of the continent's other large wild animals, including the whale, the cougar, and the musk ox—is making a comeback from centuries of human predation and habitat loss. It's now estimated one million moose inhabit North America. That they are increasing in numbers and spreading to new areas is a reminder of the moose's resilience. It's also a tribute to a new public attitude that values the possibility of simply glimpsing a big, wild animal unfettered by fences and unharried by hunters.

LEFT: *A moose can run in short bursts at 56 kilometres per hour (35 miles per hour) when fleeing or chasing off threats. But, unlike many species of deer, moose seldom jump. An adult moose depends on its long legs to step over obstacles and its size to face down most predators.*

RIGHT: *Of the planet's seven sub-species of moose—called "elk" in a nomenclature mix-up in Europe—three occupy the Eurasian continent and four are spread unevenly across North America. The moose of Alaska and the Yukon,* Alces alces gigas, *number 220 000. The moose of eastern Canada and the northern U.S.,* Alces alces americana, *number 330 000. The moose of the American Rockies,* Alces alces shirasi, *number 25 000. And the moose of the Canadian west, excluding the Yukon,* Alces alces andersoni, *number 410 000. Only A. a. andersoni is showing a small decline in population; all other North American species are increasing in numbers.*

ABOVE: *Moose are most active before dawn and usually feed relentlessly until midmorning. They then browse and ruminate and nap throughout the remaining hours of the day. In the winter, however, when a blizzard strikes, a moose such as this Alaskan bull may bed down without once moving and become half-buried in snow. It can live for long periods on the fat stored up during the prolonged feasting of summer.*

RIGHT: *Each year about 3000 collisions between speeding motor vehicles and moose occur in North America. Thousands more moose die each winter in collisions with moving trains. Moose are drawn to plowed trainlines and roads by the opportunity of easy passage during heavy snow and the salt that is sometimes used to de-ice highways.*

ABOVE: *This Alaskan bull prepares for his annual fall rut by fencing with bushes and branches in mock fights. The vegetation serves as a harmless sparring partner and burnishes the animal's antlers, removing the dead velvet of summer and shining the potentially lethal prongs.*

RIGHT: *The only time that anything passing as intimacy occurs between adult moose of the opposite sex is during the brief period of mating when male dominance has been determined and the winner gets to breed with nearby estrous females. The females roll in the male's urine-saturated wallow. They moan. They eye the bull. The bull then gently rests his head on his mate's back before mounting the cow. Within a week or so, however—as soon will be the case for these Maine moose—the liaison ends.*

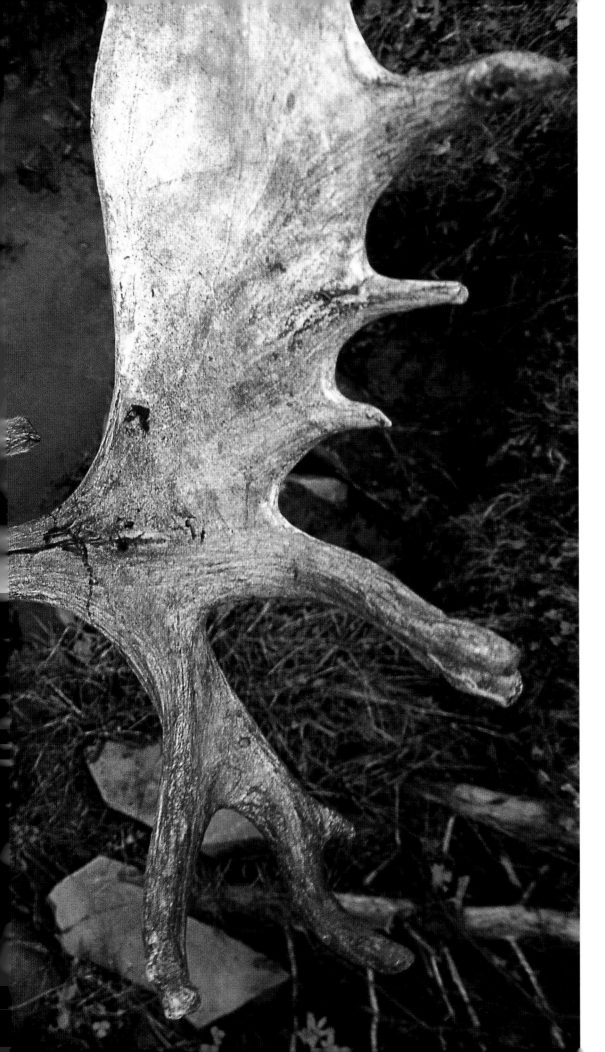

LEFT: *Bull moose begin sprouting their annual growth of antlers in April when increased amounts of sunlight affect their hormones. Cartilage grows from the males' pedicles, small knobs just above the eyes. Within just five months, the cartilage has been mineralized into bone and the antlers' fuzzy velvet falls off in bloody strips. The moose quickly scrape this off, revealing bare bone, soon polished to a fine patina for upcoming duels with other males.*

RIGHT: *This moose feeds beside an Ontario lake. Tolerating the myriad black flies and mosquitoes of the north woods, the unfussy herbivore survives by eating almost any vegetation. This includes grasses, ferns, conifer needles, deciduous leaves, wildflowers, berries, lichens, twigs, bushes, seeds, mushrooms, pond lilies, sedges, tubers, and tree bark.*

ABOVE: *A cow and her half-grown calf scrounge twigs along the edge of a northern clearing. The early Native peoples of boreal North America had dozens of names—most beginning with "moo" or "mu"—for the ubiquitous moose. The names usually referred to the moose's habit of eating twigs and bark. Today, there are over a thousand place names on the continent's maps that refer to the moose or one of its distinctive features.*

THE SEASONS

A YEAR IN THE LIFE OF MOOSE

Winter comes early and lasts a long, long time in moose country. The first snows fall in Alaska and the Yukon in mid-September and cover most of the animal's North American habitat by November. For moose, as well as most other non-hibernating northern creatures, the months ahead are a period of adversity and danger. In the wilderness, death is often winter's cold companion.

The moose is, among the continent's deer species, uniquely suited to survival in the North. Its hollow underwool of guard hairs and 25-centimetre-long (10-inch) shag of outer fur provide it protection in sustained temperatures of –40ºC (–40ºF), weather cold enough to kill an elk or mule deer. But there are other risks. By mid-December, most moose have sought out those locations that are least likely to accumulate deep snow, for the normal nutritional constraints of winter are compounded by the snowbound animals

PREVIOUS PAGE, LEFT: *A browsing moose works the bushes and low-hanging branches of trees the way a campaigning politician works a crowd. It hits on every outstretched limb, moving its head from side to side relentlessly. It clamps its mouth onto a branch and pulls it sideways between its lips, stripping off the lateral shoots and leaves. It then nips the terminal buds off—a succulent and tender dessert. Moose may stand on their hind legs to reach branches well above their heads and have been seen riding small saplings down with their chests to strip the entire tree of leaves.*

PREVIOUS PAGE, RIGHT: *During the summer, moose join other animals at natural salt licks. In the winter, however, they'll often lick the salt along icy roads and roadside culverts. This behavior, common among members of the deer family, leads to numerous motor vehicle accidents and moose fatalities.*

inability to flee predators. By this time, the bulls have shed their defensive ant-lers and the cows, often newly pregnant from the fall rut, are still encumbered with their previous spring's young. Food is scarce and often lies under a metre (39 inches) of snow. In such circumstances, moose retreat to windswept rivers and lakes, icy subalpine ridges, and plowed train tracks and roads where the snow is shallowest. They may also coalesce into small groups, hiding in thick woodland cover to protect themselves from wind chill and wolves.

As the weather worsens, moose cease moving. They lower their body tempera-ture naturally to adjust to the cold and begin using stored body fat. They may dig through the snow for buried lichens and decaying leaves or strip the bark and twigs off every tree in the vicinity. They are drawn, as well, to salted highways to replace

LEFT: *The cow-calf relationship among moose is initially very intense. By the time the half-grown moose reaches 14 months, its mother usually has a new, two-month-old calf. In a sudden and violent separation, the cow drives her yearling offspring away—head-butting and even kicking the confused juvenile whenever it tries to re-establish its maternal bond.*

the sodium acquired during the summer from salt licks and the consumption of aquatic plants. A moose's daily intake of roughage during the winter months may be only one-fifth the volume of summer's salad days. Comforts are few. In one bizarre case in Montana, a moose and her calf sought shelter in a farmer's barn during a midwinter blizzard and remained there—with the man's begrudging admiration—eating stored hay, until spring came.

Life usually isn't so generous. Winter frequently exacts a high toll on the continent's moose. The most vulnerable—the eight-month-old calves and the winter-weakened old— are picked off trying to flee from wolf packs through deep, half-crusted snow. In the far west, moose also succumb in the winter to cougars. As well, an estimated 3500 moose die each year in North America in collisions with trains and cars. (There are on record 25 human fatalities caused by motor vehicle collisions with moose.) And as winter yields to spring, some moose fall through the snow-covered ice of melting waterways and drown.

But when nature's green fuse is finally lit by the lengthening days of early April and the last snow disappears from the North's lowland valleys, the first buds swell on the dwarf birch and willow and, as if in mimic, the new antler buds swell on the heads of the male moose. The pregnant females, still trailed by their yearling offspring, begin their search for a suitable location to give birth. A dense clump of waterside bushes is good; a swamp-surrounded island, best. Both sexes gradually shed their heavy winter fur and look for a while each spring like patchy, well-worn shag carpets.

By late May or early June, depending on the latitude, the cows give birth to one or two

reddish-brown, one-metre-tall (39-inch) calves. The babies' eyes are initially rimmed with black fur. They are fuzzy and long-legged and wobbly and, if frightened, prone to bawling with a sound similar to a human child's remorseless whimpers. In other words, they're ridiculously cute. The cows lick their offspring repeatedly. The calves nurse. Within a few days, the cows prod their awkward offspring into the water, where they immediately learn to swim. The family—minus the aloof male parent—remains near the natal site for a month or two while the calves master the rudiments of foraging under the eyes of the ever-vigilant cows. The calves learn to heed their mothers' cautionary grunts and to head to the water if a predator appears.

No other animal on the continent grows as rapidly as young moose. They can put on almost a kilogram (2 pounds) a day during their first six months of life. In the carefree moments of early summer, the new calves gambol, perform splay-legged face-plants, wage mock fights with bushes, snooze, and explore like the irrepressible young of most mammal species. But predators lurk. If a cow spots an intruder, the moose attacks with a maternal ferocity that knows no bounds. Grizzlies and black bears have been observed fleeing an incensed moose cow and humans have on occasion been trampled to death when accidentally caught between an irate moose and her offspring. Even the vigilant mothers, however, can't always protect their young. In the Yukon, 50 percent of all moose calves are killed by grizzlies; elsewhere in North America, the attendant dangers of the wilderness—an unseasonable snowfall, an injury, a pack of wolves—take other young moose.

By July, the half-grown, 14-month-old moose born the previous spring receive an unexpected comeuppance from their once-doting mothers. The cows suddenly drive the yearlings off and devote themselves to their new, two-month-old offspring. The rejected yearlings,

LEFT: *The stubby protuberances on this male's head are the beginnings of its antlers. Unlike other deer species, the moose's antlers grow laterally, not vertically. In five months, they can dwarf the antler size of any other horned creature that has ever existed. Among the Alaska-Yukon subspecies, racks of 2 metres (6 1/2 feet) are common. The other three North American subspecies have smaller racks.*

PREVIOUS PAGE: *This moose, feeding placidly in an Ontario pond, is a classic icon of the North. One of the best places to see moose in North America is Ontario's Algonquin Park, where over 4000 live. In winter, they come out of the woods to lick the salted roads and in late spring every tenth bog seems to contain a moose.*

bleating tragically, try again and again to regain their proximity to their mothers, but to no avail. These young moose may trail their mothers and the new calves for months, even years, before drifting away to establish their own territory, usually nearby.

The daily life of a ruminant like the moose is circumscribed by its overwhelming compulsion to eat. And the moose is a serious eating machine. On land, it clamps its mouth onto a leafy branch or flower stem or fern and pulls, stripping off the leaves with a sliding, sidewards tug of its head. When submerged in a swamp, it may disappear for 30 seconds, only to return with a splash and a mouthful of water lily stems or tubers trailing from its lips. The unchewed vegetation is, in either case, swallowed and temporarily stored in a lobe of the moose's multi-chambered stomach for later regurgitation. In a series of 10 feeding bouts, each lasting approximately 50 minutes, followed by 50 minutes of sedentary rumination on its cud, the moose's summer days pass.

When the weather grows too warm and the deer flies and mosquitoes too numerous, moose find relief by immersing themselves to the nostrils in a cool pond. If the surrounding forage is sufficient and predators few, moose may not budge from that marshy locale for weeks. They may suction the pond bottom clear of aquatic plants. They may ride the flexible, shoreline saplings down with their barrel chests and prune entire small trees of their leaves. They may stand on their hind legs and remove all the low-hanging twigs within 4 metres (12 feet) of the ground. Researchers have calculated that some particularly complacent moose have clearcut 50 percent of all the available vegetation in their area before finally moving to a new site.

As July becomes August and August becomes September, the big bulls' thick, velvet-covered antlers grow at a phenomenal speed—1.5 centimetres (half an inch) a day, the fastest known growth rate of any animals' horn or bone. By late September, the antlers will have a use. The cows, meanwhile, are instructing their young in the gustatory possibilities of the boreal forest and the smells and sounds of approaching danger. The newly weaned calves are bulking up for the colder months of autumn ahead. During the course of their first summer, the helpless 10-kilogram (22-pound) moose babies will become hulking, 100-kilogram (220-pound) juveniles.

The summer doldrums come to an end. The willows and dwarf birch blaze in incandescent yellow along ten thousand northern creeks. Flocks of southbound sandhill cranes fly overhead in V formations. The snowline descends toward the valley floors. And moose enter a brief fall season of intense activity and socializing. Propelled by hormones and the air's chill, both sexes leave their riparian summertime retreats and head, usually upward, toward their traditional rutting grounds. Some moose migrate just 8 kilometres (5 miles). Others—such as a group of radio-collared Alaskan moose—were tracked 200 kilometres (120 miles) in their annual rutting migration to central Yukon.

The velvet on the bulls' antlers peels away and hangs for a while in grotesque ornamentation from the newly exposed and bloody prongs. The male moose bellow in a sound often compared to the lugubrious moan of a distant train passing. It can be heard from a distance of 8 kilometres (5 miles). The females reciprocate by bugling back. On at least two occasions in the past 20 years there have been cases of extraordinary misunderstanding: a lovesick bull

LEFT: *To the Native peoples of the North, the moose was—and still is—an esteemed creature. Their legends include tales of a mythic moose five times as tall as living moose. The creature could walk through over 2 metres (8 feet) of snow, and its hide was bulletproof. In centuries past, Native North Americans considered moose nose a culinary delicacy. Moose meat mixed with grease and berries and pounded into pemmican was a staple for many nomadic northern peoples.*

PREVIOUS PAGE: *In the moments before intercourse, the aroused bull repeatedly sniffs the cow to determine the timeliness of his actions. Most cows have two or three brief, 24-hour periods in early October when they can conceive. A prime bull may have a small harem of five or eight cows that he inseminates when each female comes into heat.*

was reported to have followed a whistling train into an Alaskan logging camp, and a bull in Maine became completely convinced a mooing dairy cow had seductive intentions. Usually the bulls are equally driven, but more perceptive. The males raise their heads as they move and curl their upper lips to expose a gland that detects the pheromones of nearby estrous females. The buglings and sniffings eventually draw the sexes together in localized, secure rutting grounds where dozens of moose gather. It is a situation ripe for conflict. In fact, observers in Wyoming's Grand Teton Mountains once reported eight belligerent males all eyeing each other and one anxious female.

The young males fight mock skirmishes. The large, heavily antlered bulls fight each other. Unlike the furious clashes associated with bighorn sheep or elk, bull moose engage mostly in ritual head-shaking, snorts, aborted feints, and antler-to-antler shoving matches to determine which male is the strongest. The series of battles goes on for days during late September and early October as the male hierarchy is determined. During these weeks, the bulls, absorbed in posturing and fighting, may lose 20 percent of their total weight. These clashes often produce dozens of minor puncture wounds in the combatants, but are very rarely fatal. Almost the only time they are is when two bulls' antlers lock together and the animals end up starving to death.

Once dominance has been established, the losing bulls head off in search of other males to challenge. The strutting winner excavates a wallow with his antlers, urinates and defecates in the shallow pit, then rolls in the reeking mud to acquire the distinctive wild perfume that signals dominance to the females. The cows, too, may fight each other at this

point to gain the opportunity of rolling in the winning bull's wallow. Often, one, five, or up to twelve cows may each, in turn, mate with the local dominant bull. When all the bugling, sniffing, fighting, strutting, and wallowing are done, it's mid-October. Aurora borealis dances in the cold night sky and the first rime ice appears on the dying pond-side grasses. The mating of the moose is over and each animal heads away to lower elevations for its solitary encounter with the approaching forces of winter.

LEFT: *In the Yanert Valley of south-central Alaska, a dark-eyed calf shows its coltlike legginess. The baby learns to follow its mother: wading when she wades; nibbling grass when she nibbles grass. In time, the calf's fur will lose its chestnut color and become a deep brownish-black.*

PREVIOUS PAGE: *Logging roads, seismic survey lines, and all-terrain vehicles and snowmobiles have meant the northern wilderness can now be crisscrossed by people and machines. Plowed roads are a mixed blessing for moose. They use the snow-free routes in winter. But moose have a natural tendency to stare down or even charge an oncoming threat—a reaction that may be useful when confronting a grizzly bear, but not an approaching 18-wheel logging truck.*

RIGHT: *Amid the early December snow of an oncoming Alaskan winter, a herd of moose have congregated as protection against predators. If the snow isn't too deep, the animals will scratch the ground to expose buried vegetation. When the snow cover is heavy, moose turn to bare twigs, bushes, and tree bark for nutrition. Once the snow reaches the depth of a metre (39 inches) or becomes lightly crusted, moose often cease wandering since the depth and uneven crust make fleeing a predator difficult.*

LEFT: *The clashing of bull moose is the penultimate event of the fall rut. The conflict is preceded by ritual head-shaking, roaring, mock battles with invisible opponents, and circling dances—much like the histrionic actions of participants in a World Wrestling Federation show. When the two moose combatants actually meet—not lunging at each other so much as shoving—the clack-clack of entangled antlers draws other males as spectators to the contest. The combatants snuffle and push, their breath visible in the cold autumn air. They hoof the ground and push some more. Finally, the weaker one retreats amid snorts from the winner.*

ABOVE: *In a showdown between a bear and an adult moose, the bear often comes off second best. Here, a moose—its hackles raised and eyes alert—studies a threatening grizzly after chasing it up a slope. One solid kick from the towering moose could be fatal. Bears usually retreat, hoping to find instead a young or injured moose as prey.*

RIGHT: *In the weeks before the rut, the normally solitary bulls of Alaska may travel long distances to the cows' traditional mating area, called in scientific jargon the* Umwelt. *The site is usually on a ridge or lakeshore with a good surrounding view. The male's clue to the female's location is the aromatic pheromones the cow exudes. The bulls—like this sniffing male in Alaska's Denali National Park—will pursue the scent for days or weeks until the smell suggests that the cow is ready to conceive.*

LEFT: *It's only during the fall rut or winter storms that bulls associate. Here in Wyoming's Grand Teton National Park, two members of the* Alces alces shirasi *subspecies find companionship in the snow. A moose may avoid encountering a wolf pack by lying down during a storm and letting itself become half-buried in snow.*

ABOVE: *A bull urinates into his mating wallow. He will then roll in the mud there and soon be joined by an estrous cow. Once the cow has acquired the aroma of the breeding bull, the female will defend the male's wallow against the approach of other interested females.*

LEFT: *The mid-September to mid-October rutting season involves, especially for the peripatetic Alaskan moose subspecies shown here, lengthy migrations to the traditional mating grounds. All North American male moose also face weeks of posturing and intense battles each autumn, and weeks of fasting. The whole effort culminates in an extraordinarily quick five-second mating session. The bull may repeat his efforts—with different cows—several dozen times over a period of two or three weeks.*

RIGHT: *In Alaska's Denali National Park, winter snow often lasts eight months. At the solstice there are weeks of nearly endless darkness and subzero temperatures. To survive in such conditions, moose such as this bull find a sheltered, secure place to bed down—often in a dense grove of black spruce away from the noses and eyes of predatory wolves.*

ABOVE: *As the brief northern summer ends in late August, the bull's antlers undergo a transformation. The soft velvet that has nourished the underlying bony antlers dies and shreds. The moose's behavior— fiercely scraping the antlers free of the skin—suggests the shedding is very irritating. The cleaned antlers are initially bony white, but soon acquire a brown, earthy tone as the moose continues to rake them against branches and soil.*

RIGHT: *This Alaskan cow licks moisture off her one-metre-tall (39-inch) newborn calf. This behavior appears to bond the two animals and to coax the baby to stand on its wobbly legs. Within hours, the baby has learned to follow its mother, emitting whimpers as it stumbles along. It knows to seek the mother's udder and is gently nudged in the correct direction if it mistakenly aims for the cow's forelegs. During the calf's first week of life, the protective mother never wanders more than 50 metres (165 feet) from the concealed calving ground.*

RIGHT: *Moose have an affinity for water that is equalled by only a few other terrestrial mammals. The moose is genetically adapted to temperate climates and has a low tolerance for heat, so it seeks relief from the warmth of summer submerged—like this cow—in a cool pond. Curiously, moose have no known limit to the cold they can endure.*

ABOVE: *Within a few days of their birth, calves learn one of the essential skills of moose survival: swimming. This ability is useful both as a means to reach aquatic food and to escape predators. Here, a pair of month-old twins follow their mother across a northern pond.*

RIGHT: *A cow's gestation period is about 231 days. When it's time to give birth, the animal will find a secluded location, hidden from predators. In places such as southern Alaska with quality moose browse, twins occur 75 percent of the time. In places such as southern Newfoundland with poor moose browse, twins occur only 2 percent of the time.*

FAR RIGHT: *Young moose, like these six-week-old Wyoming twins, consume milk during their first month of life, then add browsed vegetation to their diet. By the time they're this old, the calves are putting on up to 1.8 kilograms (4 pounds) daily.*

EPILOGUE

THE MOOSE
RESURGENT

From Moose Cove, Maine to Moosehorn Lake, Alaska; from Moose Jaw, Saskatchewan to Mooseheart, Illinois (home of the International Order of Moose); from Moose, Wyoming to Moose Factory, Ontario—the continent's tallest and most regal animal has insinuated itself into the iconography of the North. On the official coat of arms of Michigan and Ontario and the coat of arms of North America's oldest business, the Hudson's Bay Company, an antlered moose, standing on its hind legs like a crowned gladiator, has come to symbolize strength and persistence.

To those who have seen the moose in the wild, its appearance inevitably provokes an initial sense of awe. It *is* impressively big. But this reaction is often muted with a subsequent sense of amusement. There's something about the creature—its odd design or its impassive stoicism—that inspires giddiness, as if the Far Side creature silhouetted in the

PREVIOUS PAGE, LEFT: *On the high, mountainous plateau of Wyoming live thousands of moose like this cow—her image reflected in a pond near Grand Teton National Park. The string of parks and wilderness areas that line the American Rockies have become refuges for big ungulates and re-introduced predators such as wolves and grizzlies.*

PREVIOUS PAGE, RIGHT: *Two words some naturalists use to describe moose are "obtuse" and "stolid." This impression comes from its failure to react initially to surprise or danger. Often, it doesn't flee, but stares with ears erect, like this Alaskan cow. If it does gradually retreat, it usually stops and looks back several times, as if baffled by the intruder.*

back-country bog is a cartoon cutout, a Bullwinkle J. Moose of nature's playfulness. A hiker picnics beside Berg Lake high in the Canadian Rockies and sees something that, at first, looks like a big, drifting tree root. But the shape then resolves itself into an antlered bull swimming in the frigid, aquamarine water. The moose rises at the forested shore, cascading water, like a glistening Loch Ness monster, then disappears soundlessly into the lakeside spruce. It is almost surreal. Or elsewhere: a pair of early morning kayakers on a glassy lake below Maine's Mount Katahdin suddenly see a moose cow and her leggy twin offspring standing like statues at the lakeshore. The humans simultaneously lift their paddles and freeze. The unmoving cow and calves, their ears alert, stare back. Like the reflected images of the three moose, the moment is suspended in time.

LEFT: *These twins wait on the shore for their mother, feeding in the pond nearby. For their first months, the offspring are seldom out of sight of their attentive parent. Naturalists have often seen a cow charge an approaching bear or wolf pack, snorting, head lowered, the fur on her mane bristling, threatening to kick the intruders should they attack.*

These encounters, though still rare in most of North America, are the stuff of fireside tales for the fortunate few who have seen moose up close. But things are changing. In the past 50 years, the continent's moose population has doubled. Today, game laws and marshland protection ensure better chances of survival for the species. Fires and widespread clearcut logging of northern forests create sunny, open patches where moose fodder, such as alder, fleabane, thistles, and fireweed, thrive. Even the resurgent beaver, no longer being turned into top hats, has inadvertently helped the moose by creating thousands of new boreal ponds, full of aquatic sedge and cattails.

Currently, moose are also pushing south into the northeastern U.S., repopulating areas such as Connecticut and Massachusetts where none had survived three centuries of hunting. In Vermont, where in 1960 there were 20 moose, today there are 2000. In New Hampshire, there are now so many moose, officials have had to post "Brake for Moose" highway signs. For the first time moose are populating such places as Washington, Idaho, Colorado, and Utah, using the protection of the region's 20th-century parks and wilderness areas as their base. In 1900 there were no moose in Wyoming; a century later, the state has 14 000. This dramatic natural increase in the moose population—and the very recent reintroduction of wolves and grizzlies into the American Rocky Mountains—has propelled scientists to study the relationships between the almost fearless moose and their natural predators.

Some researchers have dressed like moose, complete with antler masks, and crept close enough to their quarry to fire slingshot-launched "scatballs," made of collected

Moose such as this ruminating female are not territorial. Like Dr. Seuss's cartoon character, Thidwick the Big-Hearted Moose, the animal is, by and large, benign, even placid. Except during the fall rut, they make little effort to defend their range. Instead, they tend to co-exist with other large game—the musk ox of northern Canada, the elk and bison of the west, the white-tailed deer across most of North America.

PREVIOUS PAGE: *A young and fuzzy Maine moose calf mirrors the posture of its mother. For now, it lives under the cow's guidance and protection, learning the ways of the wild. But in a year it will be driven away to face a largely solitary life span of 25 years or so— walking the tenuous edge between the dark woods and the sunlit shore.*

wolf and grizzly feces, to see how the animals react to the smell of unfamiliar threats. Others have donned The Full Moose, entire two-person, four-legged costumes, and walked up to moose, wagging the fake antlers, wiggling the stern, snuffling, and pawing the ground in hopes of better understanding moose communication. These researchers have reported that the animal—in properly obtuse moose fashion—has simply stared blankly at the intrusion. This unflappable nature has, on occasion, led people to believe that moose, like their reindeer relatives, are capable of domestication. In fact, in 19th-century Europe and North America, young moose were sometimes tamed and harnessed as work animals. And a 1960s Yukon family adopted a two-day-old female moose, named her Skookum, and lived with their ever-growing pet for four years before she finally wandered away into the muskeg.

But the moose's North American legacy is as a creature that once sustained—and to a certain degree still sustains—the continent's northern inhabitants and still survives as the truest emblem of northern fortitude. When a moose appears today, its presence is a reminder that, despite the incursions of civilization, something big, something almost prehistoric in appearance, something that has never learned to flee human threat still lurks at the periphery of human vision. Seen at dawn in a boreal swamp, a black shape half-shrouded in rising mist, the silent, unmoving moose is like a phantom escaped from dreams and briefly occupying human consciousness. It stands alone and enigmatically. It looks across the intervening distance, an omen of sorts, then slowly, quietly returns to the tangle of the nearby woods.

RIGHT: *On Wyoming's misty Snake River, three moose find security in numbers amid the snow. At the same time that the moose population of the New England states plummeted to near zero through habitat loss and overhunting a century ago, Wyoming was recording its first moose. Today, both regions are seeing a dramatic rise in moose numbers. New England has an estimated 28 000 moose today. Wyoming now has 14 000.*

LEFT: *A bull crosses the highway near Bow Summit in Alberta's Banff National Park. Each year in North America, more people are killed by moose—through motor vehicle accidents or being trampled— than by grizzly attacks.*

ABOVE: *A moose walking along the margins of swamps and rivers can normally maintain a pace of 10 kilometres per hour (6 miles per hour). But it must slow down, frequently turning its antlers sideways, to maneuver through dense groves of trees, like this antlered bull moving through the deciduous forest of central Maine.*

RIGHT: *On this late fall day, a cow drinks at the edge of a northern pond. As the first hints of winter occur, moose find a secure site with the potential for adequate browse. A female may spend her entire life wandering within an area no more than 8 to 16 kilometres (5 to 10 miles) from her birthplace. The polygamous males, however, may roam much farther, especially during the fall rutting season.*

LEFT: *Silhouetted in a mountain meadow at sunrise, this big, powerful bull confronts few natural threats, other than human hunters. In the 19th and early 20th centuries, moose populations across North America collapsed and most jurisdictions applied moose hunting prohibitions by the 1940s. The bans allowed the moose to recover, and today, with the population gradually rising in most places, the number of moose killed by hunters is also rising. An estimated 89 000 moose are killed annually by hunters in North America.*

RIGHT: *With Alaska's towering Mount McKinley rising as a backdrop, a bull moose overlooks a harsh, northern tundra not so different from the environment his ice age ancestors confronted when they left Eurasia 150 000 years ago. After several centuries of killing by humans—with its total North American population reduced by an estimated 50 percent by 1940—the moose is again in ascendancy. It is, in fact, spreading to new territory under the protection of newly created parks and changing public attitudes towards wildlife.*

ABOVE: *A moose stands in the steaming, warm-water swamp of northern B.C.'s Liard River Hot Springs, located just south of the Yukon/Northwest Territories border. The animal is the region's pre-eminent large creature. There are 70 000 people in northern B.C. and an equal number of moose. In the Yukon, 30 000 people and 60 000 moose share the land. In the Northwest Territories and newly formed Nunavut in the eastern Arctic, there are 25 000 people and 40 000 moose.*

LEFT: *It is not difficult—on close observation—to see the illustrative, if not the comedic potential of the moose. After a visit to the Maine woods, 19th-century naturalist Henry David Thoreau called the moose "singularly grotesque." Moosehead Beer, bottled in Canada's Maritime Provinces, features a moose on its logo. The 1990s CBS-TV series* Northern Exposure *ran its credits over a moose ambling through an Alaskan town. Hockey star Mark "Moose" Messier is not the only athlete to be nicknamed after the creature. Most people are amused by moose because—like the rhino or the manatee—the animal is so ugly it's cute.*

SUGGESTED READING

Addison, Ray B. *North American Moose Conference and Workshop*. Ministry of Natural Resources, Ontario, 1973.

Bauer, Erwin A. *Antlers: Nature's Majestic Crown*. Stillwater, Minnesota: Voyageur Press, 1995.

Franzmann, Albert W. and Charles C. Schwartz. *Ecology and Management of the North American Moose*. Washington, D.C.: Smithsonian Institute Press, 1998.

Hoshino, Michio. *Moose*. San Francisco: Chronicle Books, 1988.

Petersen, David. *Racks: The Natural History of Antlers and the Animals That Wear Them*. Santa Barbara: Capra Press, 1991.

Peterson, Randolph L. *North American Moose*. Toronto: University of Toronto Press, 1978.

Silliker, Bill, Jr. *Moose: Giant of the Northern Forest*. Toronto: Key Porter Books, 1998.

Stelfax, J. Brad. *Hoofed Animals of Alberta*. Edmonton, Alberta: Lone Pine Press, 1993.

Van Wormer, Joe. *The World of the Moose*. Philadelphia: J.B. Lippincott Co., 1972.

Whitehead, G. Kenneth. *Deer of the World*. London: Constable and Co., 1972.

INDEX

Bold entries refer to photographs.

PHOTO CREDITS